# Gwathmey Siegel

# Gwathmey Siegel

## BY STANLEY ABERCROMBIE

# MONOGRAPHS ON CONTEMPORARY ARCHITECTURE

WHITNEY LIBRARY OF DESIGN, an imprint of Watson-Guptill Publications/New York

**GRANADA** London Toronto Sydney New York

Copyright © 1981 by Stanley Abercrombie

First published 1981 in New York by Whitney Library of Design,
an imprint of Watson-Guptill Publications,
a division of Billboard Publications, Inc.,
1515 Broadway, New York, N.Y. 10036

**Library of Congress Cataloging in Publication Data**
Abercrombie, Stanley.
   Gwathmey Siegel.
   (Monographs on contemporary architecture)
   1. Gwathmey Siegel Architects.   2. Architecture,
Modern — 20th century — United States.   I. Title.
II. Series.
NA737.G95A83      720'.92'2      81-11442
ISBN 0-8230-7257-6         AACR2

First published in Great Britain 1982 by Granada Publishing
Granada Publishing Limited—Technical Books Division
Frogmore, St Albans, Herts AL2 2NF
and
36 Golden Square, London W1R 4AH
117 York Street, Sydney, NSW 2000, Australia
100 Skyway Avenue, Rexdale, Ontario M9W 3A6, Canada
61 Beach Road, Auckland, New Zealand

ISBN 0 246 11737 0

Granada®
Granada Publishing®

Manufactured in U.S.A.

First Printing, 1981

Edited by Sharon Lee Ryder, Stephen A. Kliment and Susan Davis
Designed by Robert Fillie
Set in 11 point Spartan Light

# Contents

# Introduction

# The Art of the Evident

"I can explain all the poems that ever were invented," Humpty Dumpty told Alice, "and a good many that haven't been invented just yet." Such ability is in great demand these days, but, for the works of Gwathmey Siegel, no Dumptian skills will be needed. Current architecture suffers a plethora of allusions to be traced, ambiguities to be weighed, and contradictions to be contemplated, but Gwathmey Siegel buildings seem to rise clear of most internal jitters and exterior dependencies. They constitute an opera independent of its libretto, a poem independent of explanation. It really is wonderfully refreshing: what you see is what you get.

Which is not to say that everything can be seen at a glance or that these are buildings lacking in subtlety. Not at all. But they are the ends — the whole ends — of Charles Gwathmey and Robert Siegel's creative process. There are no diagrams that must be studied for understanding them, and our appreciation of them depends not at all on our recognizing references to The Strip or recalling details of the Viceroy's House. Gwathmey and Siegel are not at work in a cultural vacuum, of course, and their buildings could not have been designed without some precedents we shall name, but the buildings speak to us directly, not in code.

## GUIDES AND DIRECTIONS

The first work of Charles Gwathmey to have some national recognition was a shingled beach house on Fire Island. The house's plan focused on an interesting central room, around which was placed a pinwheel of subsidiary rooms, but the exterior was — to be generous — unassuming. In its distinction between "served" and "servant" spaces and in its clear articulation of parts, the house was an expression of concerns that dominated the University of Pennsylvania school of architecture under Louis Kahn, a major influence on Gwathmey, who was at Penn from 1956 to 1959. Perhaps it was even a catharsis of those ideas, for they never appeared again quite so literally in Gwathmey's work. Other early influences whom Gwathmey acknowledges from his Yale years (1959 to 1962) were James Stirling, Shadrach Woods, Paul Rudolph, and Vincent Scully. Having spent the same years at Pratt and at Harvard, Robert Siegel names as influential in his own study William Breger, Sibyl Moholy-Nagy, and Aldo Van Eyck.

In 1966 Charles Gwathmey produced a suddenly and unmistakably mature work: the house and studio for his parents (a painter and a photographer) in Amagansett, Long Island. The little pair of buildings became one of the most familiar works of the '60s and '70s, an instant icon. They were fresh, those houses, with a look all their own. Naturally there was a scramble in the next few years to place them in historical context. Sibyl Moholy-Nagy noted that Gwathmey and Richard Henderson, his partner until 1970, were "devoted admirers of Le Corbusier, whose influence, going back to Garches and the Villa Savoie, is clearly visible." Robert A. M. Stern said the houses combined "influences from Le Corbusier and from the American shingle style." Jaquelin Robertson observed that "Ed Barnes is successfully wedded to Corb here, bearing an independent child — no mean feat." And Manfredo Tafuri (in *Five Architects*, where the houses were shown) asked, "Are we in the presence here of a special East Coast subculture compounded of European abstraction and American technique?"

Well, yes and no. Whether or not there was justification for identifying an East Coast subculture, we were certainly in the presence of just the synthesis Tafuri named, a synthesis pioneered in the earliest American houses of Marcel Breuer. The Breuer work, for all its idiosyncrasies, is a crucial precedent for later work in which the Bauhaus masters' houses of Walter

Gropius meet New England vernacular. And the wood houses of Gwathmey and Siegel (partners since 1971) bear a surface resemblance to the early works of that synthesis: flat walls of vertical tongue-in-groove siding punched by carefully considered openings, busy asymmetric compositions somewhat steadied by sculptured fireplace elements (although not anchored by them in a Wrightian way), and hardware (as in Corb's work) of nautical extraction. There is also a working relationship, through Edward Larrabee Barnes, of the three firms: Barnes was a Breuer student at Harvard and then an apprentice in Breuer's office; Gwathmey and Siegel were both apprentices in Barnes' office in the mid-'60s.

But the differences are more significant than the similarities. A Breuer building is often an assemblage of parts, put together with wit and an eye for surprising juxtapositions — wood against masonry, panels of primary color against natural materials. A Barnes building is more uniform, more static, an impressively still object in the midst of a world in flux. Gwathmey Siegel, working in a manner radically different from either Breuer or Barnes, manage to combine in single works a playfulness worthy of Breuer with a presence worthy of Barnes. For their buildings, even their large buildings, are coherent unities, uniform in materials (almost completely of wood, almost completely of brick, etc.) and with interiors related to exteriors, plans to sections, opaque forms to transparent ones — all without interruption or deceit. But there is more in Gwathmey Siegel's work than this heightened unity; the unities are electrically alive with movement. Gwathmey Siegel give us the "push and pull" of a Hans Hoffman painting, but in three dimensions.

In the best of their work, a highly personal sense of space seems to pervade the whole building — sometimes even the whole neighborhood around a building — marking out chunks of earth and air in a three-dimensional grid. Most building elements, vertical or horizontal, snap into this grid, and such is the nature of the personal physics governing here that it often exerts a negative magnetism when corners are turned: as opposite charges attract, so an opaque element in one plane seems to call for a transparent one at right angles. There are circular elements, of course, with their centers always at grid intersections, and there are some pianolike shapes segueing from one grid line to the next, but these are just embellishments on the basic theme.

There are obvious and often-noted resemblances between Gwathmey Siegel's work and the early work of Le Corbusier. They share the use of Platonic geometry, the "free plan," and the "free facade," and in the Cogan house there is almost a direct quotation from the Villa Stein at Garches. But in concept, despite appearances, the Le Corbusier work that is closest to Gwathmey Siegel's work is the chapel at Ronchamp — absolutely whole, dynamic, volumetric, and plastic.

We can also see the influence of Mies — not, to be sure, of his idealized, universal symmetries, but of his fiercely asymmetric early works, with their busily alternating solids and voids and their reluctance to change planes without changing materials. Another influence, pointed out by Ulrich Franzen, is the work of Frank Lloyd Wright, both in the articulation of interiors, using built-in furniture as a secondary architectural system, and in the extension of buildings into the landscape. Site-ordering compositions for Gwathmey Siegel's Kislevitz, Weitz, and Cincinnati houses are, in Franzen's words, "reminiscent of Frank Lloyd Wright's elaborate systems of pergolas, porches, podiums, and garden walls radiating out from the house itself, such as the Coonley house gardens or the outdoor spaces of Taliesin West." The occasional flickering into physicality of an always underlying geometry, the intersections, alignments, and sometimes unexpected subtractions of parts have something in common as well with the cerebrations of Gwathmey Siegel's fellow "Fiver," Peter Eisenman.

But Gwathmey Siegel demand of their geometric manipulations a simultaneous functional purpose: program is a primary determinant of their buildings, not only in the general layout of spaces and circulation patterns, but also in detail — what will the view be, where will the light fall, which way should the door swing, where will the piano be played and the napkins stored? We are, in this sense, far removed from Eisenman's abstraction and approaching the eighteenth-century rationalism of Carlo Lodoli and others. In the words of his friend Francesco Algarotti, as translated by Emil Kaufmann, Lodoli insisted that "nothing shall show in a structure which does not have a definite function." Gwathmey and Siegel do not pursue functionalism to any of its lunatic extremes — they do not confuse utility with morality, nor do they see fitness to use as the prime source of beauty — but they do follow it as far as most orthodox modernism has done. Unlike many of their contemporaries, Gwathmey and Siegel refrain from using building elements that are merely signs, symbols, or allusions, preferring those that, while sometimes evocative, also "have a definite function."

Both on this functional level — the program made manifest — and on the level of the dominating grid — pervasive, abstract, and personal — Gwathmey Siegel's concerns are most clearly demonstrated in their residential work, where the incidence of change and modification are most frequent, the particularities most dense. For this reason, as well as for the more usual appeals of vicariousness and voyeurism, the firm's residential work has received disproportionate attention. The present collection, while not neglecting the value of that work, attempts to redress an imbalance by including a majority of larger, nonresidential works. The same principles can be seen at work there, and with the same success.

## MODULAR COHERENCE

The exact nature of the Gwathmey Siegel grid deserves attention. It is based on Le Corbusier's Modulor, but it is the Modulor demystified. In the houses for Gwathmey's parents a 4'-0" grid had been used in plan, and in the Strauss house of 1968 (Purchase, New York, by Gwathmey with Richard Henderson) a 6'-0" grid was tried, but in all later work a 3'-6" grid has ruled. This has been found to be highly accommodating of most programmatic demands: with 6" taken away for structure, the 3'-0" dimension is a good stair width or door width ("You won't find any 2' doors in our buildings," Siegel says). This is also close to the 113 centimeter (cm) dimension (3'-8½") that Le Corbusier calls the "single unit": the distance from the floor to an ideal man's solar plexus and the basis of the Fibonacci series of numbers Le Corbusier calls the "red" series. The "double unit," 226 cm (or 7'-5"), is the distance from the floor to the tips of the fingers on a man's upraised arm and is the basis of Le Corbusier's "blue" series. Gwathmey Siegel's nearest equivalent, based on multiples of 3'-6", give or take another 6", is 7'-6" (229 cm) — quite a comfortable, even cozy, height for minor rooms — and for major rooms a double height of 16'-0" (489 cm) — comprising 7'-6" plus 7'-6" plus 1'-0" for intermediate structure — seems important without being absurdly grand.

With repeated use, the grid has come to serve Gwathmey Siegel not only as a tool that makes pleasing proportions and consonant forms practicable, but also as a tool that provides shortcuts in the design process. From experience, the architects know that one dimension in the series will produce a rail height that a seated person can look over and that another dimension

produces a rail height too high to be looked over; they know the grid units that are needed for elevators, shower stalls, beds, closets, and desks; they know what equipment and storage space a two-unit-long kitchen will hold or what a three-unit kitchen will hold. As a Japanese would know instinctively the area of a six-tatami or ten-tatami room, Gwathmey Siegel are liberated by familiarity with the module from the most tedious, small-scale design decisions and free to concentrate on decisions both larger scaled and more abstract. As Siegel puts it, the module lets them "jump the level of design beyond that of subitems."

There is also a less pragmatic, more philosophical justification for using the grid: Gwathmey and Siegel feel there is something genuine in the claims that the Modulor is based on dimensions of the human body and that it therefore produces results perceived as appropriate for people; they do not, however, follow Le Corbusier in rambling on about the branching of twigs, the proportions of the Campidoglio, or the paintings of Cezanne. In any case, the grid they employ works for them.

## DIFFERENTIATION BY COLOR

In the firm's earliest work the materials of the building shells — usually cedar siding or, as at the Purchase dormitories, modular masonry units — were left natural, sometimes contrasted inside, as in the Steel houses, with white cabinetwork and a white fireplace element. As Robert Stern wrote of those works (in contrast, for example, with the contemporary works of another "Fiver," Richard Meier), they had "not succumbed to the impossible dream — the dematerialized structure of wood painted white." But, later, there was a change: as Gwathmey Siegel came to work on a series of interior design commissions, for which their control of the building shell was limited or nonexistent, they began to investigate the use of color as a substitute for three-dimensional manipulation. Its use as a substitute soon led to its use as a supplement to form and, finally, to a use of color as an important part of an architectural vocabulary rooted in — but expanding upon — modernism. Color is now an established factor in the work of Gwathmey Siegel. Exterior building shells, once natural wood or brick, are now frequently white; in some commercial structures, a light brown travertine has been used; and, in the case of the Long Island house, some exterior framing and chimney elements are to be brightly colored. Inside the buildings, a varied palette of pale or strong colors (the choice affected by the quality of the site's natural light) now prevails.

## AMBIGUITY IN MIRRORS

Relative to Gwathmey Siegel's increased use of color is their addition of reflective and translucent materials that add glitter and an element of visual indeterminacy to their geometric contexts. An early precedent for this was the use of a bewildering array of projected lights and images in Gwathmey and Henderson's 1968 Electric Circus, a New York dance hall that was a sensation of its day, but less eccentric glitter was introduced in Gwathmey Siegel's 1976 Shezan restaurant. The materials used for this effect include mirrors, polished aluminum ceiling tiles, and, most noticeable, glass block; black and white photomurals have also been used at times to similar effect. The applications are, primarily, those building types for which some degree of glamour and fantasy was wanted — hair salons, restaurants, retail spaces — but also include, to a lesser extent, residences, banks, and offices. As in the case of color, these materials bring to Gwathmey Siegel's work a visual enrichment, an element of delight, and an intentional ambiguity that embellishes the work while stopping short of any overt decoration.

## WHOLES AND PARTS

Developments in the use of grids and colors are details, of course. The most interesting changes in the work of Gwathmey Siegel are those that have taken place in the exploration of the firm's primary esthetic concern (one of the most primary of all esthetic concerns): the contest between the whole and its parts. Repeatedly, it is this contest that lends Gwathmey Siegel compositions their tension, and the contest has been fought in many ways. To begin with, there were the tight, unified objects of Gwathmey's parents' houses and the classical solid of the Cogan house, its assertive parts only incidents within a stable envelope. At the end of a chain of experiments there comes the fractured composition of the Cincinnati house, its elements dangerously near the limits of the gravity that would bind them together. Then, at last, in the Long Island house that closes this selection, there is a return to consolidation. But it is a consolidation of parts grown much

more varied and independent than were the parts of the earliest compositions. It marks, perhaps, the beginning of a new cycle, the upward progress in a spiral leading — who knows where?

## CONCEPTS INTO BUILDINGS

But we leave to Humpty the explanation of poems, both those built and those not yet invented. For, despite this work's richness and the multiplication of its foci, it remains work of remarkable and agreeable accessibility. As Gwathmey has said, ". . . what we make is almost totally understandable by anyone once he sees it; viewers get completely involved with it immediately."

One reason for its accessibility is that these are designs meant to be built: they accept an obligation to be reasonable, both for their builders and for their users. There have, certainly, been a few Gwathmey Siegel designs that, so far, remain unbuilt — the very interesting Geffen house in Malibu, a couple of houses in New Jersey, the housing complex for New York's Roosevelt Island — but there has never been a Gwathmey Siegel design not *meant* to be built. Commonplace as that is in the mainstream of architectural practice, at a time when some gifted and influential architects, such as Eisenman and John Hejduk, seem indifferent to construction of their designs, and at least one architect, Leon Krier, actually expresses animosity toward construction, a love of building deserves notice.

A reasonable corollary of passion for building is care for detail, and here, as well, the work of Gwathmey Siegel is exemplary. It is well-informed about the nature of materials and how they fit together, how they move, and how they weather. Typical is the detailing of the recently completed Cincinnati house: here, provisions for heating and air conditioning have been kept visually minimal, but, when seen, they are exquisite; room-width cabinet tops from single pieces of white oak fit within plaster walls with infinitesimal tolerances; and tile joints in bathroom walls align exactly with tile joints in bathroom floors. Such concern for execution, Gwathmey and Siegel understand, is important to the success of an architecture that is a self-contained, self-sufficient artifact rather than a reference to other buildings or other times.

Perhaps their buildings owe some of their straightforward immediacy to the two partners' working habits: no fey fancy could survive for long at the single worktable Gwathmey and Siegel have shared for a decade. They have never had private offices, they say; in matters of design, they may never even have had a private thought. This is not a team of an esthete with a technician, or of an architect with a businessman; it is a pair of designers, each constantly testing the other.

The work of Gwathmey Siegel — not to explain it, but to characterize it — is carefully conceived, it is well built, and through a conscientious process of design development, the built result is the direct, consistent embodiment of the concept and is remarkable for its lack of elements extraneous to that concept. Gwathmey and Siegel do not bother to build what might better be drawn or written. With high standards and with energetic exploration of possibilities, these architects have developed an architectural vocabulary that confirms the promise of some fundamental aspects of modernism and that simultaneously promises something else: the continuing and increasingly personal expression of the firm's own particular vision.

# Projects

# Tolan House

In 1971, four years after the completion of the house and studio for Gwathmey's parents, the firm designed this house immediately west of them in Amagansett, New York, on Long Island. The two older elements and this larger new one face each other on an open field; there are a few scattered trees, but not enough to obscure visibility. The new building has, therefore, been made wholly compatible with the old in both geometry and materials (the walls, outside and in, are of tongue-and-groove cedar siding, treated with bleaching oil). Yet it has been given an identity of its own by means of its siting at an angle different from that of either older building and, most definitely, by means of a powerful wall paralleling the property line and enclosing the long side of a tennis court. (It was intended to enclose as well a small guest wing beyond the tennis court, but this was not built).

Within the intentional similarity, the new work shows a heightened spatial complexity and some relaxing of the strictly Platonic geometry employed four years earlier. At the corner nearest the older buildings, for example, a billiard room bows forward in a curve that, while a segment of the circumference of a cylinder, is only a small segment of that circumference. It is juxtaposed, moreover, to a half-cylinder of different radius and with a different center, the combination suggesting a looser relationship of parts than in the earlier houses. A further development is that some building elements here — the east-facing entrance wall, for example — are presented, at least in part, as two-dimensional screens rather than as surfaces of three-dimensional solids.

Functionally, the plan divides spaces into a linear children's wing and a taller, more cubic adult area, the two meeting at a circulation "knuckle" comprising the entry and a stair up to the living-dining area on the second floor (where it enjoys a superior view). Compositionally, the Tolan house might seem extremely mannered if seen alone, but seen as an addition to the existing composition of the Gwathmey house and studio, it appears appropriate and rational. The important wall forms a stable backdrop for the pirouetting of the two earlier houses, and beyond the wall, the new house is glimpsed as a third distinct character but one with recognizable family traits.

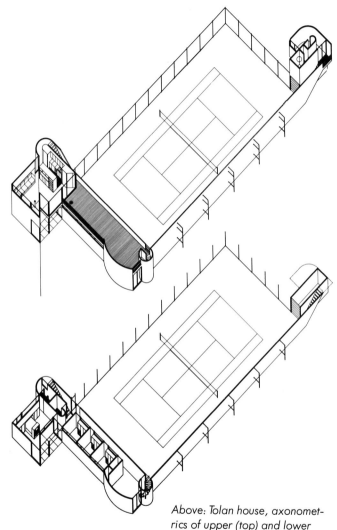

*Above: Tolan house, axonometrics of upper (top) and lower levels.*

*Right: Tolan entrance facade, an early Gwathmey Siegel experiment in ambiguity. Like all parts of the Gwathmey house and studio, this can be read as part of a geometric solid, but it can also be read as a transparent screen fronting a more solid element.*

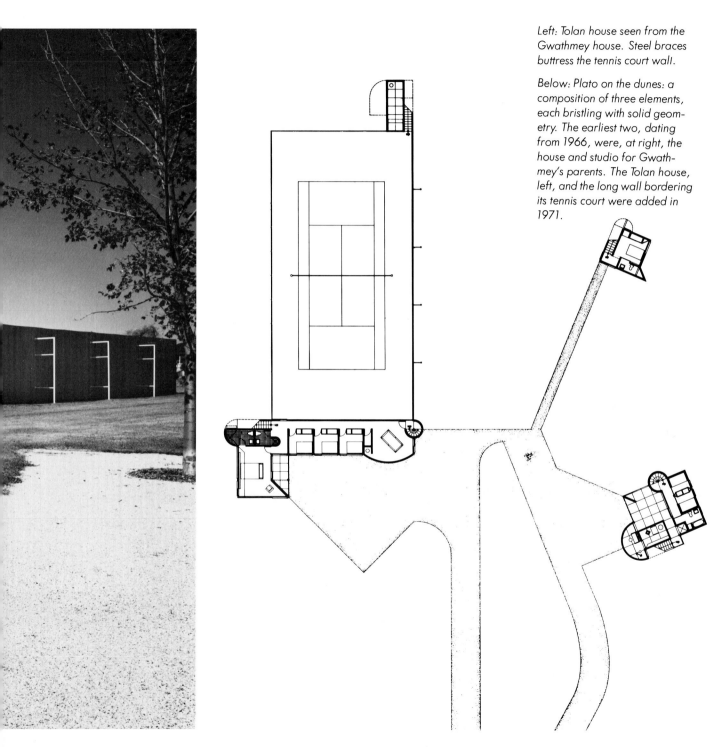

*Left: Tolan house seen from the Gwathmey house. Steel braces buttress the tennis court wall.*

*Below: Plato on the dunes: a composition of three elements, each bristling with solid geometry. The earliest two, dating from 1966, were, at right, the house and studio for Gwathmey's parents. The Tolan house, left, and the long wall bordering its tennis court were added in 1971.*

Roof deck attached to Tolan entrance facade; living area beyond; tennis court to the right.

White cabinetwork within the natural cedar shell constitutes a subsidiary architecture. In later work of Gwathmey Siegel these colors will be reversed, but visual distinction between house scale and furniture scale will be maintained.

# Whig Hall

Although the Gwathmey Siegel firm has undertaken many interior design commissions, there are only two instances in their work so far of building renovation so radical that it finds strong expression on the exterior. One is the 1976 Kislevitz house, contained in a "Spanish" shell; the earlier, and the more vital, is the 1972 adaptation to new uses of Princeton's Whig Hall, originally built in 1893 to designs of A. Page Brown. (The building is still the home of the Whig debating society, but now there are additional facilities for public and university use.) Although Whig lacks the nuance that Gwathmey Siegel had learned to exercise by the time of the Kislevitz design, the earlier building has a robust athleticism the later building lacks. Whig's neoclassical demeanor, which has, after all, something to do, however secondhand, with literate and controlled architecture, presents a much more interesting context — a much stronger adversary — for new forms than does the flabby pseudovernacular of the Kislevitz shell. The result at Whig is thrilling, poignant, a real debate. Manfredo Tafuri reacted this way: "In the belly of academic purity there lives the dawning nucleus of the avant-garde: this is what the surprising assemblage of Whig Hall wishes to express metaphorically." And there is, indeed, something about Whig Hall that has the shock value of exposed entrails within a classic frame of base, column, and entablature. There is also, in the abandonment of eyes-front symmetry for a new directionality, a response to the site, opening the side of the building that parallels a campus path, keeping the opposite side intact.

The program called for 10,000 sq ft (930 m²) of area in a building that originally had only 7,000 (651 m²). Obviously, new construction within the shell was necessary. Four floors have replaced the original three (although the main lecture hall has been given a double height), and the new structural system, independent of the masonry shell, has been kept independent of most interior partitions as well and expressed as regular punctuations of a Corbusian "free plan."

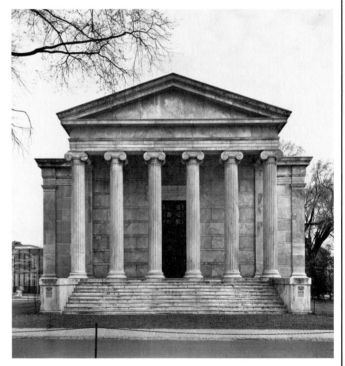

The front facade of Princeton's Whig Hall as it looked in 1893 (above) and the side facade as it looks now (right) demonstrate the extent of Gwathmey Siegel's 1972 remodeling. The result is an exhilarating contrast between classical shell and modern content.

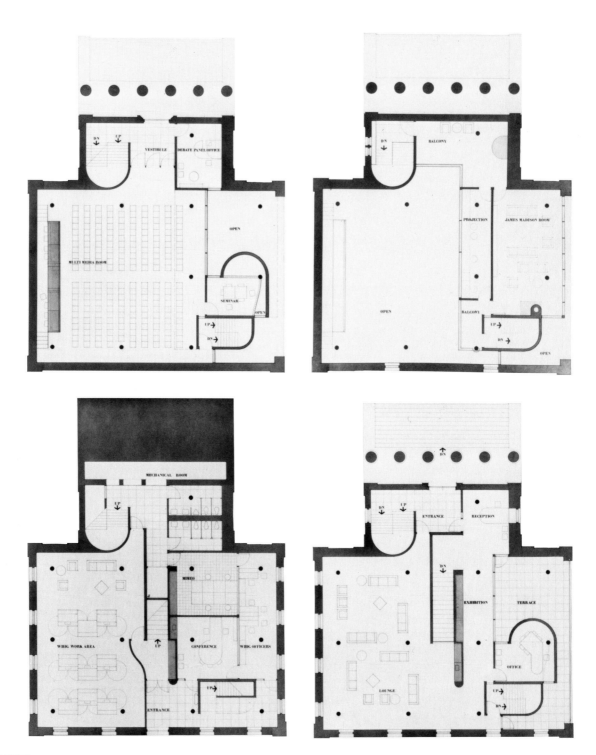

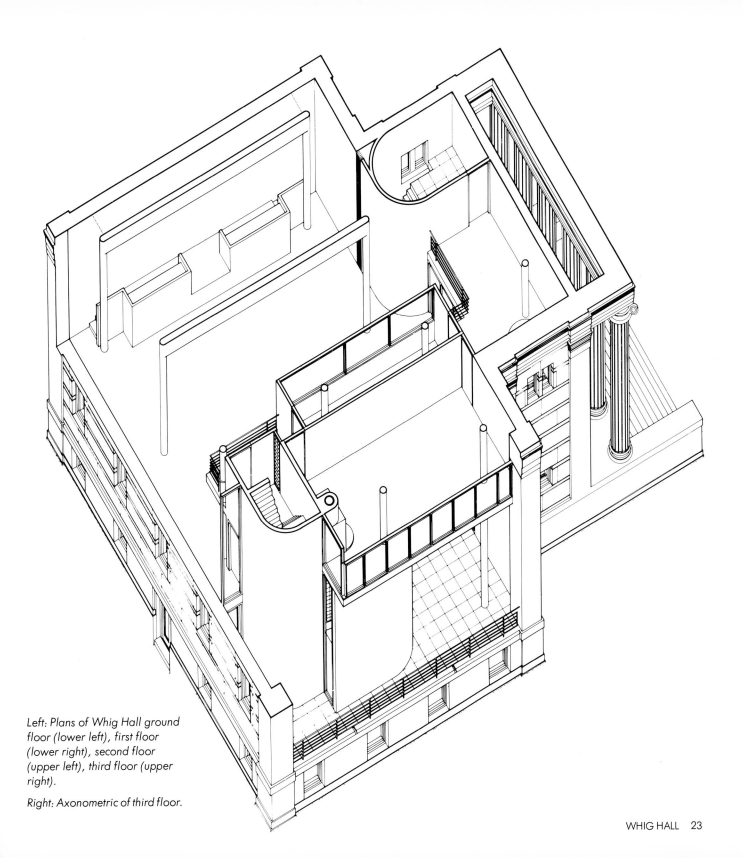

*Left: Plans of Whig Hall ground floor (lower left), first floor (lower right), second floor (upper left), third floor (upper right).*

*Right: Axonometric of third floor.*

*Left: Skylit stairway with pipe rails in Whig Hall.*

*Above: Piano-shaped seminar room seen from below.*

*Right: Lecture hall.*

# Cogan House

A key design in Gwathmey Siegel's work, the Cogan house composition is dominated by a single rectangular solid from which other forms are eroded or projected. A comparison with Le Corbusier's Villa Stein is natural. Here, as there, the main living quarters are lifted above grade to a *piano nobile* — in this case, to give them a view over the East Hampton dunes to the sea — and this fact is emphasized on the seaside facade, though not on the relatively uncommunicative entrance facade. On both sides, largely solid projections with rounded ends contrast pleasantly with the flat but largely transparent or cut-away surfaces of the main block. Interior spaces are given vitality by the introduction of three long ramps, with opposing slopes, linking the four levels. A compound curve at the edge of the double-height living room adds a lyrical gesture.

In some ways, the Cogan house is an all-new residential version of the Whig Hall renovation, which was being designed at the same time in 1972. Here, as there, we see a stable, classical form that contains — or, in this case, partly contains — a much more active subsidiary composition. Here too, as at Whig Hall, there is a combination of two structural systems, an overall bearing-wall structure bracketing a self-sufficient column grid, with interior partitions freely arranged within the bearing walls and about the columns. The whole composition expresses dynamism within stability, and the expression is so clear and felicitously executed that the Cogan house must be considered one of the firm's finest accomplishments — cogent, confident, and delightful.

*Below: Among Gwathmey Siegel's residential work, the Cogan house of 1972 is perhaps the most clear and the most classical, but it presents classicism with a difference: a reposeful overall form invaded and enlivened by lyrical subsidiary elements. South facade shown here.*

*Right: Living area; skylit ramp at left.*

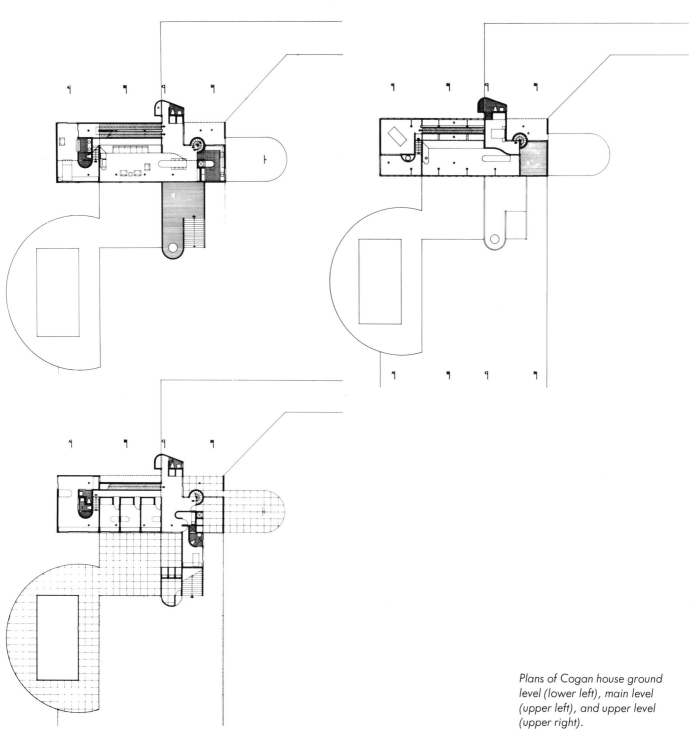

*Plans of Cogan house ground level (lower left), main level (upper left), and upper level (upper right).*

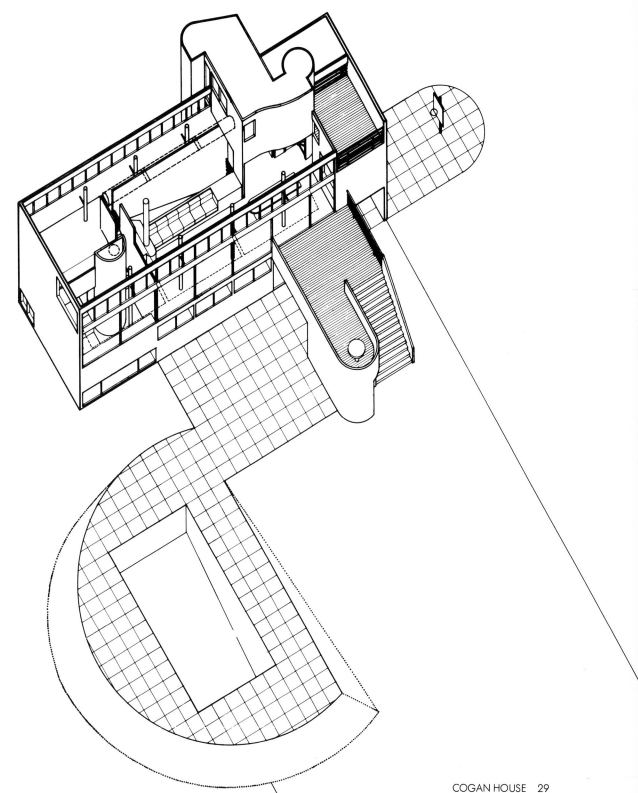

*Axonometric.*

*Left: View from Cogan dining area.*

*Below left: North facade.*

*Right: Curved deck, with dressing rooms below, projects from the rectangular body of the house.*

# Purchase Dormitory

The 800-student dormitory of the State University of New York at Purchase was the first large-scale commission of the firm in 1973, but it betrayed no lack of self-confidence, and despite some critics' predictions, the formal vocabulary first used at Amagansett proved to be thoroughly valid for bigger statements. As the campus plan (by Edward Larrabee Barnes) required, the dormitory presents an orderly linear facade to the central mall; the other side, facing away from the mall, is more free, open to the fields beyond, and richer in formal variations. These last include partly cylindrical projections that enclose stair towers or—in four larger elements—student lounges. The basic range of dormitory rooms is varied, but regular: a basic plan repeated 40 times. Freestanding within the U-shaped range is an elaborately sculptured dining hall-library building. As dictated by the master plan, the entire building group is faced with a modular clay unit, although some soldier courses covering prefabricated lintels give the walls a textural variety some of the neighboring buildings lack, and the material is used here as bearing-wall construction rather than (as at other campus buildings) as a veneer.

*Right: Section of typical dormitory range on the Purchase Campus.*

*Below: Dining pavilion at left; typical dormitory wing at right.*

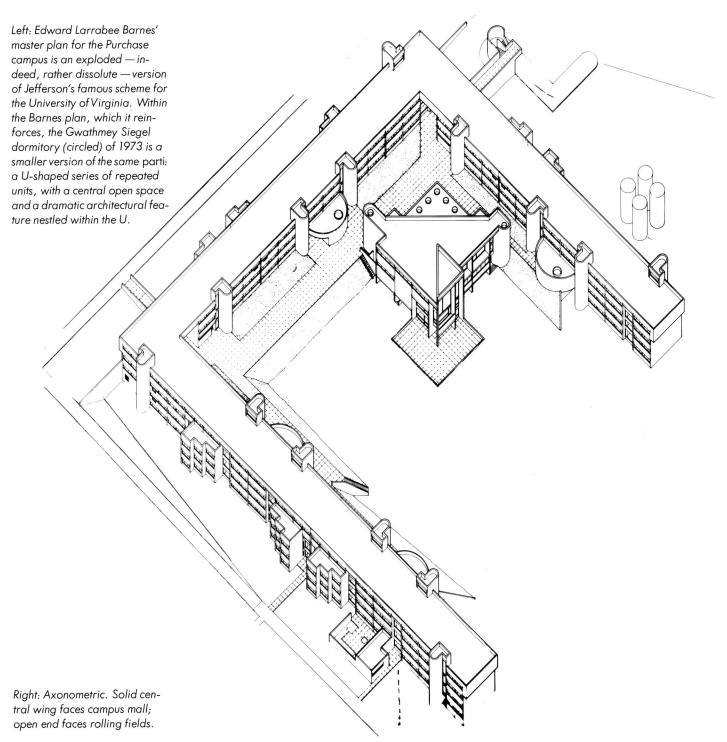

*Left: Edward Larrabee Barnes'
master plan for the Purchase
campus is an exploded — indeed, rather dissolute — version
of Jefferson's famous scheme for
the University of Virginia. Within
the Barnes plan, which it rein-
forces, the Gwathmey Siegel
dormitory (circled) of 1973 is a
smaller version of the same parti:
a U-shaped series of repeated
units, with a central open space
and a dramatic architectural feature nestled within the U.*

*Right: Axonometric. Solid cen-
tral wing faces campus mall;
open end faces rolling fields.*

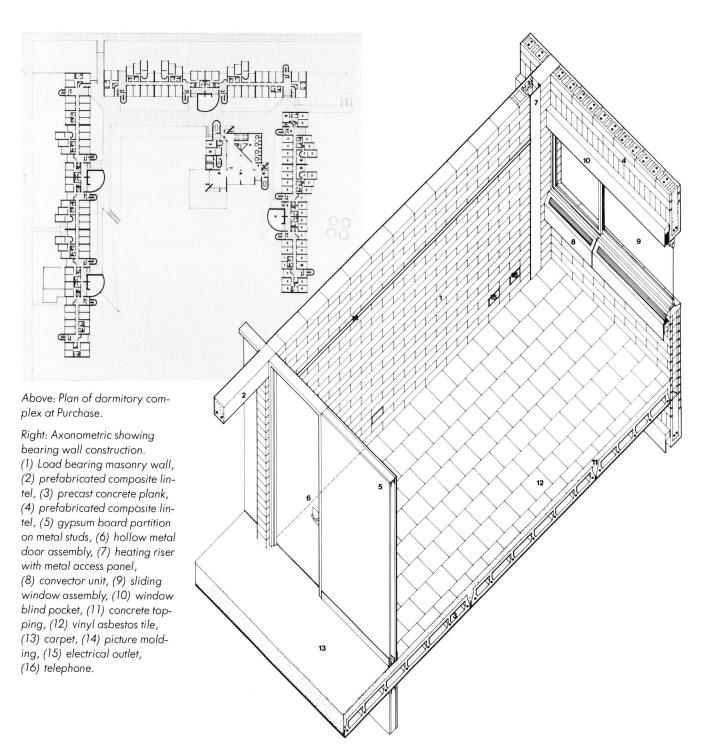

*Above: Plan of dormitory complex at Purchase.*

*Right: Axonometric showing bearing wall construction.*
(1) Load bearing masonry wall, (2) prefabricated composite lintel, (3) precast concrete plank, (4) prefabricated composite lintel, (5) gypsum board partition on metal studs, (6) hollow metal door assembly, (7) heating riser with metal access panel, (8) convector unit, (9) sliding window assembly, (10) window blind pocket, (11) concrete topping, (12) vinyl asbestos tile, (13) carpet, (14) picture molding, (15) electrical outlet, (16) telephone.

Corner projection. Small rounded elements contain stairs; the larger one holds a student lounge.

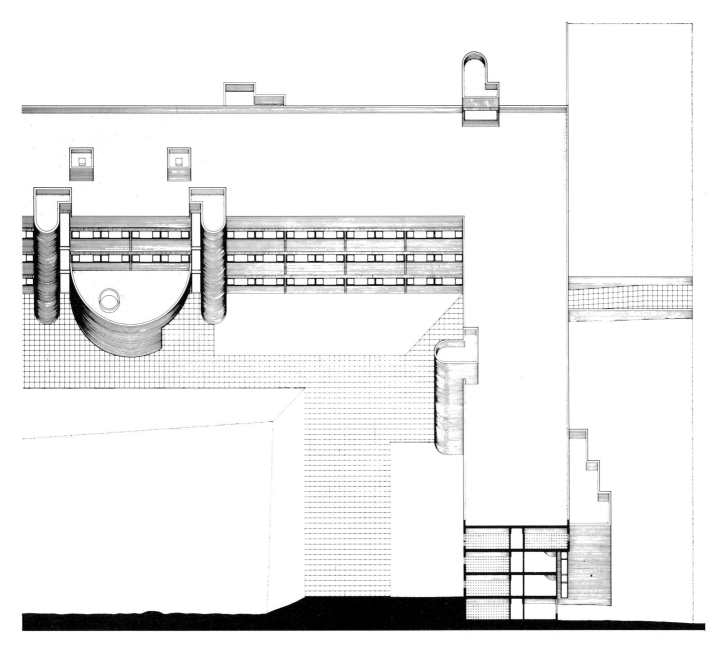

*Left: Dining hall in central pavilion of Purchase dormitory as seen from mezzanine.*

*Right: Mezzanine lounge overlooking dining hall.*

# Pearl's Restaurant

Gwathmey Siegel's tricks with mirrors began in a bold and effective way with their renovation of a Manhattan storefront space into Pearl's restaurant in 1974. The infill, as in the case of Whig Hall, is both uncompromisingly new and respectfully related to the building facade around it, but without Whig Hall's brash exuberance. This exterior plane is also a direct expression of the new interior volume: a low rectangular space opened to a high barrel-vaulted one. (Only half the vault is built; it is completed by its own reflection.) A strong yellow panel — the color of Chinese mustard, for this is one of New York's best Chinese restaurants — originally filled the end of the vault. In a later modification this panel has been mirrored, visually extending the vault and removing an unpopular back-of-the-room stigma that the most remote tables seemed to have, but also removing a very pleasant spot of color. The seating plan in the long, narrow space provides a promenade for the sport of customers watching other customers, and the kitchen, also necessarily long and narrow, has been designed with a logical one-way circulation pattern. The result is clear and efficient, but with — because of the ambiguity and glitter of mirrors, clear glass, and glass block — a dash of exoticism.

*Right: The street facade of Pearl's restaurant in New York, designed in 1974, telegraphs the shape of the interior volume beyond it and also relates the new construction to its immediate context.*

*Below: Street level plan.*

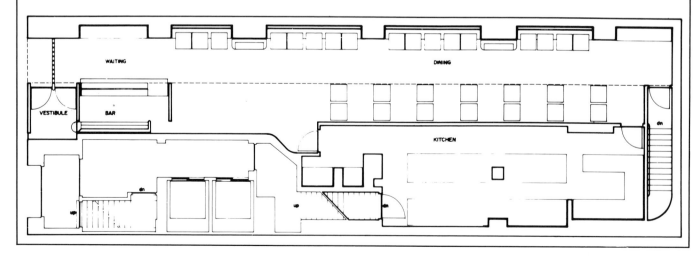

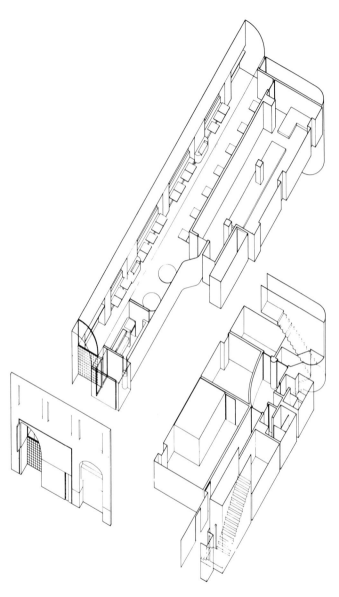

*Above: Axonometrics of Pearl's facade, upper (top) and lower levels.*

*Right: Looking toward the rear of the restaurant. The mirrored wall suggests a completion of the vaulted volume.*

# Perinton Housing

The earliest of several Gwathmey Siegel residential communities, Perinton, near Rochester, New York, is a classic — almost a diagrammatically pure — manifestation of the planning principle of separating vehicular and pedestrian traffic, a principle at least as old as Clarence Stein's Radburn plan of 1929. This principle has led the designers to organize the 560 units (garden apartments and townhouses built in 1975) along four parallel vehicular culs-de-sac, the units' major rooms facing away from the traffic and opening to green areas and to a pedestrian path leading to a 6,000-sq-ft (558-m²) community center at one corner of the site. Occasional modifications of the basic pattern, accommodating atypical green areas, and the stepping of units to meet changing grade conditions add variety. Even so, such a generalized solution necessarily lacks the verve of more specific solutions for specific users.

*Below: The Perinton, New York, housing of 1975 is a clever, although severe, expression of planning distinctions: habitable areas separated from service areas; automobiles separated from pedestrians. Here units are stepped down to fit grade changes.*

*Right: Elevation detail. The abstract composition of panels and openings is reminiscent of early modern work such as Walter Gropius's masters' housing at the Bauhaus.*

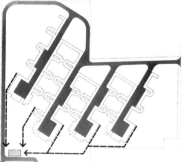

*Left: Site plan. Vehicular traffic (shaded area) is kept distinct from pedestrian paths (dashed) that lead to the community facility at lower left.*

*Above: Aerial view of Perinton housing complex.*

*Right: Upper (top) and lower levels of typical units.*

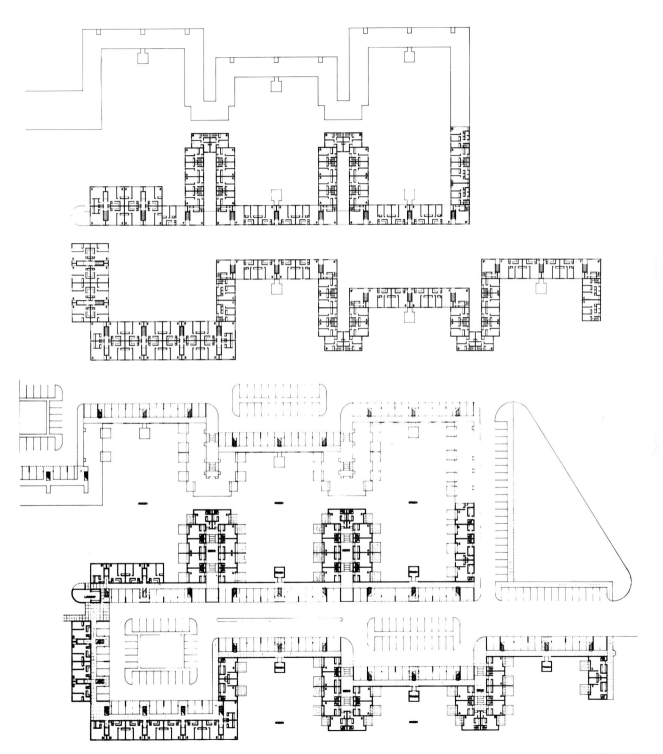

*Left: Parking beneath units in the Perinton housing complex.*

*Above: View of interior garden area.*

# Shezan Restaurant

The spatial ambiguity of Pearl's restaurant is made more complex and diffuse in the multilevel underground spaces of Shezan, basically three major rooms divided by glass block partitions and entered from street level by a calculatedly indirect series of stair runs and turns. Polished aluminum ceiling panels add a new element of reflectivity, as does a scattering of metal drum tables. Flooring is beige travertine; many walls are carpeted. The total effect is a psychological transformation from the everyday world above to a place apart.

There is more to this 1976 transformation than the commonplace desire for restaurant atmosphere; there was a real need, in the case of Shezan, for subterfuge, because awareness of the actual spatial condition — continued progression, lower and lower, into a basement — would have been depressing. Gwathmey and Siegel contrive here to move diners to ever lower depths without their awareness. They achieve this by means of visual ambiguities and also by positive action: at each point where vertical movement occurs, they have provided an important horizontal attraction — an important wall, an important volume of space, or both.

Similarly, lighting has been devised to detract us from the fact that the basement has no natural light. The warm flicker of a hundred candle flames is repeated in the room's reflective surfaces, including those overhead. The total effect is more of being under a starry sky than of being under a Manhattan building, more of floating than of being buried. Shezan is a tour de force of environmental manipulation.

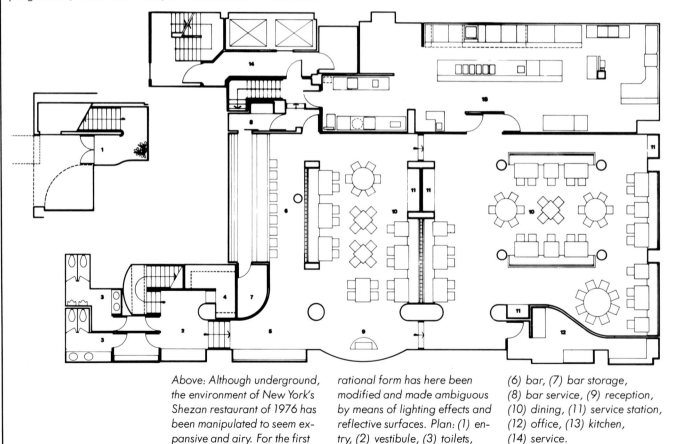

*Above: Although underground, the environment of New York's Shezan restaurant of 1976 has been manipulated to seem expansive and airy. For the first time in Gwathmey Siegel's work, rational form has here been modified and made ambiguous by means of lighting effects and reflective surfaces. Plan: (1) entry, (2) vestibule, (3) toilets, (4) coat check, (5) lounge, (6) bar, (7) bar storage, (8) bar service, (9) reception, (10) dining, (11) service station, (12) office, (13) kitchen, (14) service.*

*Right: Entrance at street level.*

Left: Descending to the restaurant.

Right: Banquette in Shezan's bar area, with semicylindrical reception desk beyond.

*Left: Bar and upper tier of dining area in Shezan.*

*Right: Lower tier of dining area.*

# Vidal Sassoon Salon, Beverly Hills

Gwathmey Siegel have done a series of hair salons for Sassoon—big ones, small ones, all in different configurations, but all with a consistent image and a consistent color palette (browns, grays, and silver). In these salons, as in some of the firm's restaurants and in their Poster Originals Gallery in New York, an element of fantasy is appropriately present. This is provided by the use of reflective surfaces—not only mirrored wall surfaces, but also polished aluminum ceiling panels.

At the 1977 Beverly Hills salon shown here there are details, as in all the salons, that reinforce the reflective character, notably a pair of mirrored wall surfaces interrupted at eye level for galleries of photographic images, producing a combined effect that is quite surreal. With some striking larger photomurals, all monochrome, and with some glittering walls of glass block, the reflectivity dissolves the typical Gwathmey Siegel forms into less coherent, intentionally theatrical ones, but without resorting to the application of decorative frills.

Like Pearl's, but quite unlike the salon's neighboring storefronts on Rodeo Drive, the facade does not present expensive goods (or even images of expensively styled hair) but displays its own interior volume. The entrance is clearly indicated, as is the double-height space beyond. This is a store as a world apart, with a storefront as a sign telling the way.

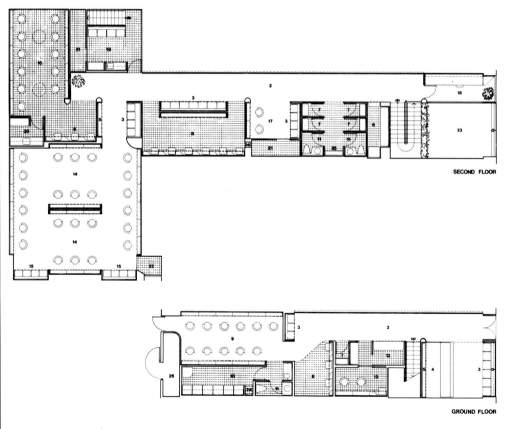

SECOND FLOOR

GROUND FLOOR

*Right: Ambiguity and theatricality through the use of reflective surfaces characterize the Vidal Sassoon salon in Beverly Hills of 1977. The form of the reception area is expressed in the street facade.*

*Left: Floor plans: (1) entry, (2) gallery, (3) waiting, (4) reception, (5) display, (6) coats, (7) dressing, (8) washing, (9) cutting (men), (10) laundry, (11) toilets, (12) appointments, (13) VIP, (14) cutting (women), (15) drying, (16) tricology, (17) hair test, (18) manager, (19) staff, (20) dispensary, (21) storage, (22) street display, (23) open, (24) laundry chute, (25) public telephones, (26) mechanical.*

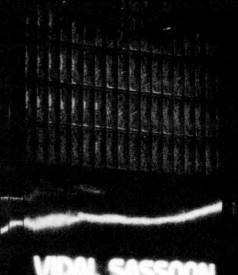

*Left: Mirrored wall with eye-level photographs.*

*Above: Shampoo area in Vidal Sassoon salon.*

# Swid Apartment

In their freestanding residential work and, where appropriate, in commercial buildings as well, Gwathmey and Siegel generally make a clear distinction (usually by means of color and finish) between elements at building scale and elements on the scale of furniture and cabinetwork. This distinction adds a further degree of interest to the buildings, allowing the smaller elements, observed independently, to be seen as metaphors for the enveloping larger ones. In the case of interior renovations, of course, the opportunity for such distinctions is diminished, there being few enveloping elements subject to the architects' control. For the Swid apartment in New York, completed in 1978, certain storage units have been treated as natural wood furnishings set within larger, apparently more structural features, but the treatment here is necessarily ambiguous at times. Further visual enrichment and complication come from the palette of paint colors used here, in addition to white and natural wood surfaces.

The forms of the Swid apartment are the most lyrical to appear in Gwathmey Siegel's work to date. Such a great number of curved niches and sweeping piano-shaped forms have been employed that the whole apartment, it seems, is caught up in an almost audible waltz.

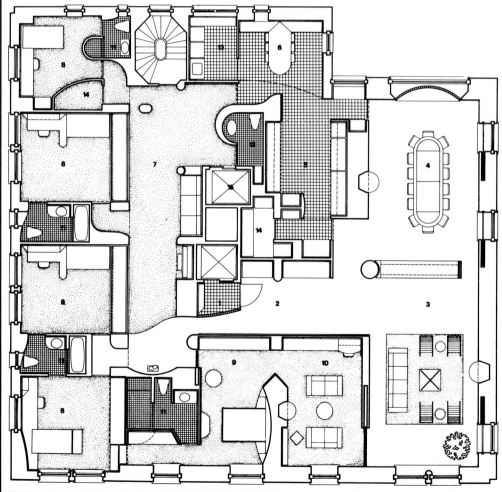

*Right: The Swid apartment renovation of 1978 is dominated by curved forms; here elevator foyer opens into gallery.*

*Left: Plan: (1) entry, (2) gallery, (3) living, (4) dining, (5) kitchen, (6) breakfast room, (7) playroom, (8) bedroom, (9) master bedroom, (10) study, (11) bathroom, (12) powder room, (13) laundry, (14) storage, (15) service elevator.*

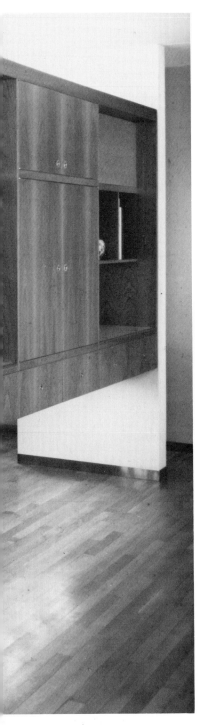

*Left: View from gallery through wall unit that separates Swid living and dining areas.*

*Right: Kitchen; opening at right leads to playroom.*

*Below right: Master bedroom.*

Left: Playroom area in Swid apartment; bedrooms are beyond cabinetwork at right.

Right: View from hall into the master bedroom suite of the Swid apartment. The elevator entrance is behind the glass block wall at left.

Color Portfolio

SWID APARTMENT    65

Color Portfolio

# Color Portfolio

Left: In the 1971 Tolan house, the living room is placed on the upper level, giving it a view over the dunes to the sea; it also looks towards the well-known 1966 house and studio for Gwathmey's parents, to which it is — compositionally, although not functionally — an addition. (For the complete Tolan project, see pages 14—19.)

Right: The Cogan dining area, looking toward double-height living room. (See pages 26—33 for a review of the entire project.)

## Color Portfolio

*Left: Looking toward the street in the half-vaulted dining area of Pearl's restaurant. (See pages 40–43 for a more thorough treatment of the project.)*

*Right: The lower-level dining room of Shezan of 1976. Great care has been taken to prevent awareness of the restaurant's basement location. (For more about this project, see pages 50–55.)*

## Color Portfolio

*Above: Night view of the south facade of the 1980 Cincinnati house, dominated by a partly detached brise-soleil. (See pages 102–107 for a review of the entire project.)*

*Left: Daytime view of south facade.*

*Detail of southwest corner of the East Campus dormitory complex at Columbia University, completed in 1981, showing pedestrian mews at left. (For the complete project, see pages 108– 113.)*

# Knoll, Boston

Although Gwathmey Siegel have often undertaken interior design commissions, this example of urban infill is rare in their work. The site is a particularly cherished shopping street in a city particularly sensitive to such matters: Newbury Street, just off the Public Garden, in Boston. It is a fine street of small shops and galleries, but its architecture is a mixture of sizes, styles, and ages; certainly not all Newbury Street is of landmark quality. Great care had to be taken, nevertheless, to make the new work of 1980 compatible with both the neighborhood and with the Knoll image (not to mention the Gwathmey Siegel image). A building-high panel of glass block, lighting a stair, is interrupted by horizontal strips that do not actually align with the new building's floor levels but do align with floor levels of the older buildings to its right. A projecting element on the ground floor is curved (as are the bow windows common in the area) and flush with the structure at the left, while the main block is flush with those at the right. Large glass areas on the three lowest floors (the ones used by Knoll) are inconsistent with the older buildings, but these areas are recessed. The top three floors (now used as rental area) have a more traditional void-to-solid ratio. Interior spaces are understated backgrounds for furniture display, but these are modulated by terracotta-colored columns, divided by a stair climbing a warm gray wall, traced with white pipe rails, and distinguished by a second-floor semicircular enclosure of glass block and by a neon strip on the soffit.

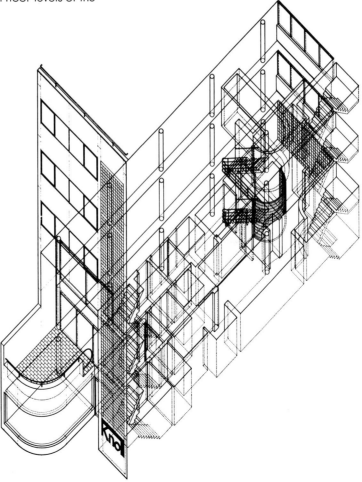

*Left: Ground floor showroom area of 1980 Knoll building in Boston.*

*Right: Axonometric.*

Left: Knoll showrooms and offices in Newbury Street setting in Boston to which the design is thoughtfully related.

Right: Roof terrace above the curved ground floor projection serves as display space for outdoor furniture.

Below right: Entrance with projecting display element.

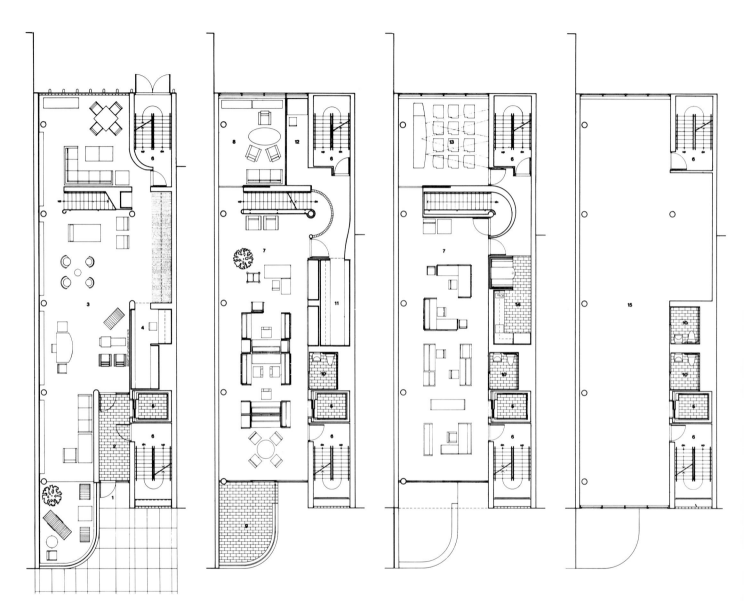

Above: (From left to right) Knoll ground floor, second floor, third floor, and fourth to sixth floor plans: (1) entry, (2) lobby, (3) reception/showroom, (4) samples/workroom, (5) elevator, (6) firestairs, (7) systems showroom, (8) manager's office, (9) terrace, (10) toilet, (11) storage/workroom, (12) Xerox/mailroom, (13) projection/meeting, (14) kitchen/lounge, (15) typical lease floor.

Right: Second floor showroom area beyond stair with neon lighting strips.

# Weitz House

In the body of Gwathmey Siegel work to date, the composition of this 1978 beach house at Quogue on Long Island is atypically complex in relation to its size. It is really two linked houses — a minor one for guests, with garage below, and a major one for family spaces (and, tucked beneath it, a second guest suite). This is no simple binuclear scheme, however, for the two elements, each almost square in plan, are overlapped and interlocked at their corners. Further, the two blocks, from the entrance approach, have been given quite different characters: the larger block an imposing near-symmetry (so far as the overlap will allow), the smaller one a more typical asymmetry. And there is also a level change, accomplished just at this "knuckle" — the entrance grade, with pool and tennis court, on a level below the dunes beyond. The dramatization of vertical circulation is a favorite Gwathmey Siegel pastime, but seldom has it seemed so crucial, so much the heart of a design, as in this house. It is thus a wondrously kinetic house, compared with the others, as well as an ingenious little cabinet packed with clever passages.

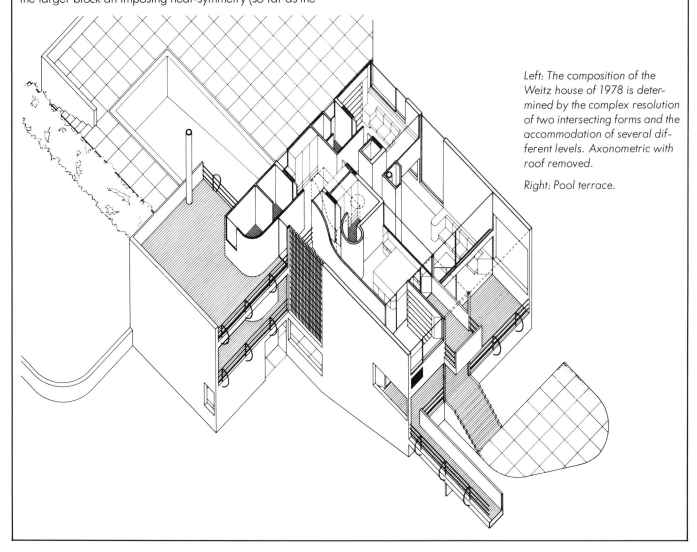

*Left: The composition of the Weitz house of 1978 is determined by the complex resolution of two intersecting forms and the accommodation of several different levels. Axonometric with roof removed.*

*Right: Pool terrace.*

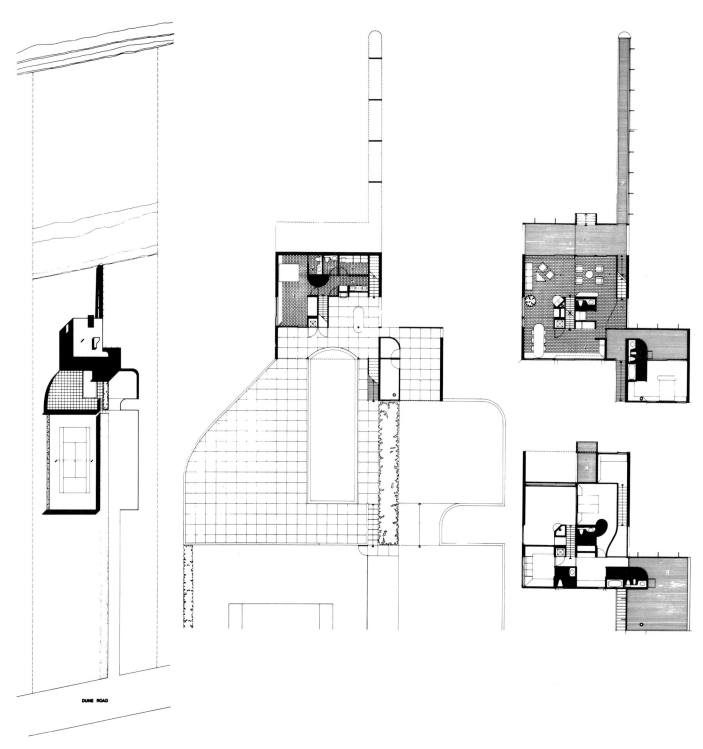

DUNE ROAD

*Opposite page, left: Weitz site plan.*

*Opposite page, middle: Ground floor plan.*

*Opposite page, left above: Detail of main floor plan.*

*Opposite page, left below: Detail of upper level plan.*

*Right above: East elevation of Weitz house.*

*Right: Entrance facade.*

*Left: Corner fireplace in Weitz living room.*

*Above: Master bedroom and stair down to main floor.*

*Right: View toward ocean beyond living room and deck.*

# Geffen Apartment

Of all Gwathmey Siegel designs, perhaps the play of geometry is at its tightest density in this relatively small Manhattan apartment of 1979. The vocabulary of forms here (with the exception of a rather organic tub enclosure in the master bathroom) is quite limited, without the compound curves of the Swid apartment. The grid used here is not a repetitive one in the typical Gwathmey Siegel manner, but its spacing is varied to meet a great range of new and existing conditions, and this network of organizing lines is displayed quite clearly as joints in the marble flooring. Typical of the apartment's complex geometry is the detail above the main rooms' window walls: a cove for indirect lighting curves downward above a projecting shelf, its front surface cut back at a 45-degree angle and its soffit mirrored.

*Right: Gwathmey Siegel geometry at its tightest: the 1979 Geffen apartment in New York. View into den from living room.*

*Left: Plan: (1) elevator vestibule, (2) entry, (3) gallery, (4) living, (5) dining, (6) den, (7) bar, (8) master bedroom, (9) dressing, (10) bathroom, (11) guest, (12) kitchen, (13) powder room, (14) service.*

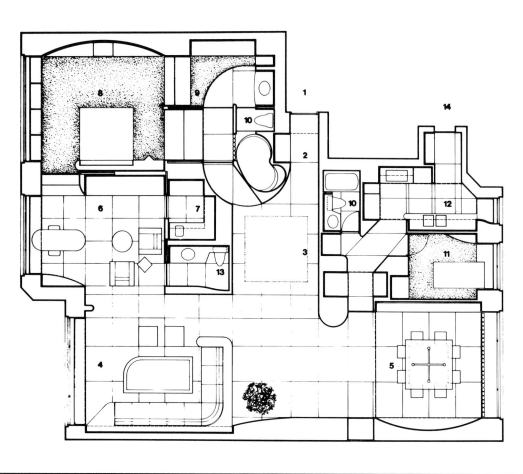

*Left: Den with cantilevered desk in Geffen apartment.*

*Right: Living room, looking toward dining room.*

*Below right: Living room with oak cabinetwork.*

Left: Master bedroom.

Above: View from Geffen entrance gallery toward master bedroom.

# Thomas & Betts Headquarters

A 160,000-sq-ft (14,880-m²) corporate headquarters for a manufacturer of electrical components in Raritan, New Jersey, the Thomas & Betts building of 1979 is a good example of Gwathmey Siegel's formal inclinations modified — but not overwhelmed — by the program and budget limitations of suburban commercial work. Gwathmey and Siegel feel that buildings of any size, to be understandable to their users, need, at the least, a major space to which all other spaces can be related. In some large-scale work, they have employed courtyards (or, in the current work at Columbia University, a cloister) for this purpose; in their houses, circulation elements have often performed the same service.

Circulation is also the referential element at Thomas & Betts: a skylit double-height circulation gallery that culminates in the building's two main entrances (and the parking beyond) and that also serves the stairs and all parts of the building's relatively small percentage of public areas. The appended dining hall became an opportunity for a large two-story volume. A photomural by Charles Nesbit covers one wall; the opposite wall has been given the flourish of a slight curve.

*Below: For the Thomas & Betts headquarters building of 1979, a two-level circulation spine serves as an organizing element. Ground floor plan (left): (1) entry, (2) lobby, (3) gallery, (4) office space, (5) laboratory, (6) dining, (7) serving, (8) storage, (9) toilets, (10) mechanical, (11) service. Upper floor plan (right): (1) balcony, (2) office space, (3) mechanical, (4) toilets, (5) open.*

*Right: Entrance lobby.*

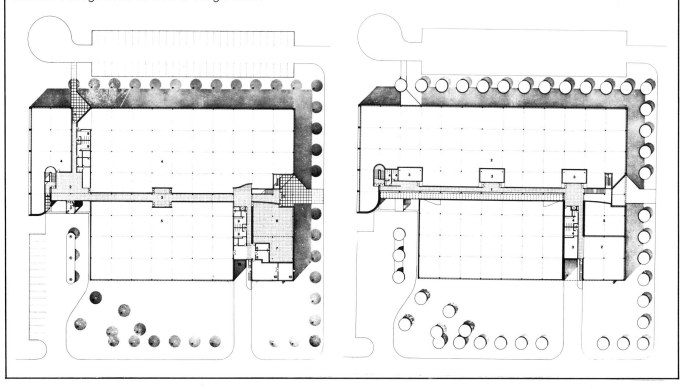

Left: View of Thomas & Betts building from northwest.

Above: Detail of visitors' entrance.

Right: Detail of skylit double-height gallery.

Left: Upper level of Thomas & Betts gallery.

Above: Stair at employees' entrance.

Right: Dining hall with Charles Nesbit photomural.

# The Evans Partnership Building & Offices

The Evans office is a commission within a commission, a 5,000-sq-ft (465-m²) interior design for the owner's own space within the shell of an existing speculative office building, also a Gwathmey Siegel design. The overall building in Parsippany, New Jersey, has a powerful presence and sense of luxury, with its travertine-faced fin walls welcoming entrance into an arcade from parking areas at both sides and bracketing a serene reflecting pool. Uncharacteristic of Gwathmey Siegel's work, it is very simple and perfectly symmetrical. The office interior, completed in 1980, seeks to compensate for the fact that it is largely interior space. A skylight admits natural light, and walls of glass block — some flat, some curved — play games with it. Two sizes of block are used, 6 in. (15.2 cm) square and 12 in. (30.5 cm) square, and the differences afford interesting variations of texture and ambiguities of perspective. Mirrored walls and reflective ceilings add further visual richness.

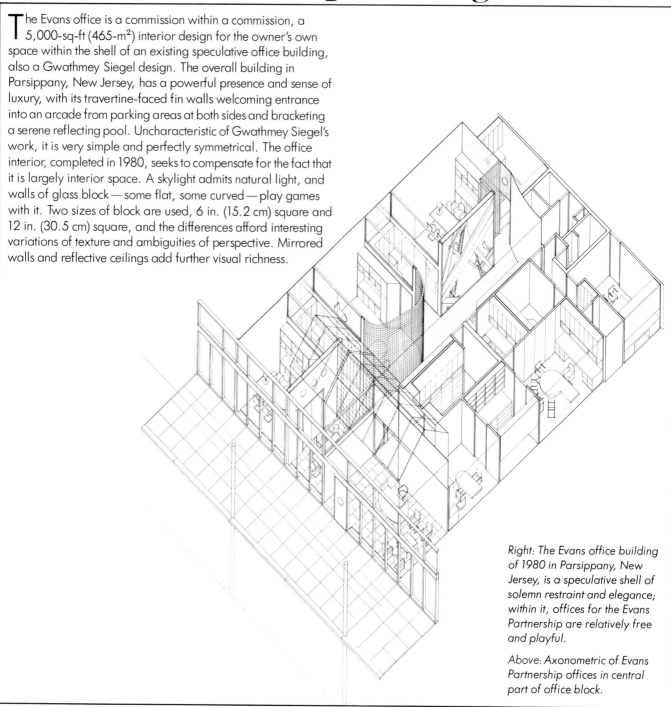

*Right: The Evans office building of 1980 in Parsippany, New Jersey, is a speculative shell of solemn restraint and elegance; within it, offices for the Evans Partnership are relatively free and playful.*

*Above: Axonometric of Evans Partnership offices in central part of office block.*

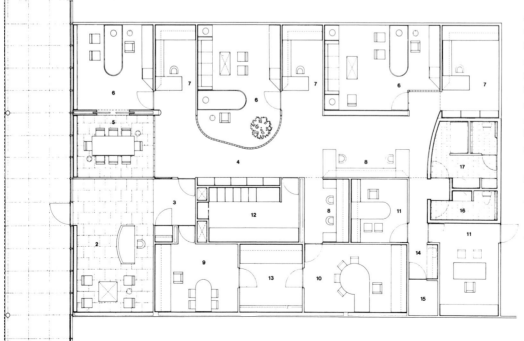

Left: Plan of Evans Partnership offices: (1) arcade, (2) reception/waiting, (3) vestibule, (4) gallery, (5) conference, (6) executive offices, (7) executive secretaries, (8) secretaries, (9) estimator, (10) construction manager, (11) construction foreman, (12) file room, (13) plan room, (14) kitchenette, (15) storage, (16) men, (17) women.

Above: Entrance arcade and reflecting pool.

Right: Night view of Evans Partnership office beyond reflecting pool.

Left: Secretarial area with photomural.

Right: Detail of Evans executive office.

# Cincinnati House

The 1980 house near Cincinnati represents an extreme in one line of development within Gwathmey Siegel's work, a development toward controlled dispersal and fragmentation that has as its opposite the compact packaging of the 1972 Cogan house. Charles Gwathmey and Robert Siegel refer to the house's similarity to a village, a cluster of small units, and there is such a quality about the composition. Nevertheless, the parts of the house are related in direct, not at all haphazard, ways — solids aligned with solids, or solids aligned with voids — and all parts are tied together with an attenuated and important circulation spine that swells, at its ends, into study and sitting areas. (The most remote part of the composition, a small guest wing beyond a tennis court enclosure, has not yet been built.)

An ambiguity about the dominance of parts versus the dominance of the whole is suggested by the brise-soleil of the main wing. This wing, containing kitchen, dining and living rooms, and the master bedroom suite, is, in any case, the largest element of all, and it has been given the most dramatic siting, near the edge of a hill dropping away to a long view of the Ohio River valley. The brise-soleil, made to read from some angles as a freestanding element, although it is not, further emphasizes the main wing's importance and its focus on the view and seems to ignore the presence of other parts of the composition: it relates only to its own wing, not to any other elements or to the composition as a whole. Its freestanding appearance is further negated by its use as a container for an upper-level screened porch, an indoor/outdoor volume that extends above roof level, thus involving even the roof deck in the play of interlocking volumes.

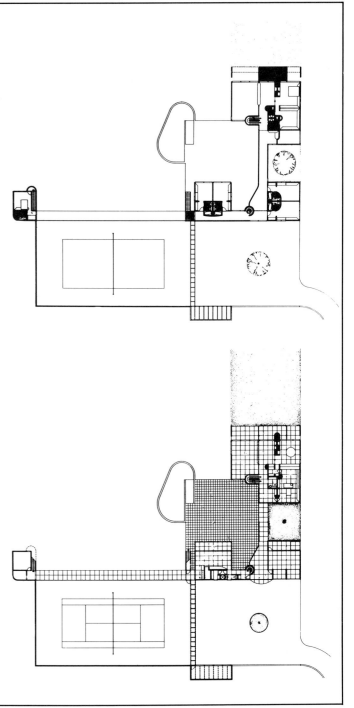

*Right: For a large house near Cincinnati, Gwathmey Siegel have designed a deceptively rambling "village" of elements that are nevertheless carefully related to each other and linked by a single upper-level gallery. Ground floor plan (below). Upper level plan (above).*

*Opposite page: Southeast corner of main wing beyond pool.*

*Left: East facade of Cincinnati house, with greenhouse at right.*

*Below left: View into courtyard from covered entry walk.*

*Right: View south from living room.*

Left: Study area overlooking breakfast room in Cincinnati house.

Above: Double-height living room seen from study area at end of upper-level gallery.

Right: Sitting area at end of upper-level gallery.

# East Campus Complex, Columbia University

Just completed in the spring of 1981, the Columbia complex is, at first glance, an absolutely straightforward solution to a tricky problem of relating a large new building volume to a smaller-scaled, older context. A low wing of dark brick corresponds in size and color to its neighbors; beyond an interior courtyard, a much taller slab, perched on the steep cliff that falls into Morningside Park, enjoys splendid views of the city and accommodates the larger part of the complex's dormitory space for 665 students. The lower floors of the highrise, by a change of brick color, also acknowledge the cornice line of neighboring buildings.

Further examination, however, shows this to be an intriguingly intricate urban complex, its intricacy only hinted at by its richly patterned fenestration. The program is enriched by the inclusion of a number of nonresidential uses, primarily a Humanities Center closing the north side of the courtyard. The dormitory facilities themselves have been arranged in a variety of unit types — single rooms, flats, duplex and triplex apartments — interlocked in an elaborate split-level building section.

Similarly, the courtyard is much more than a source of air and light at the heart of the complex. Punctuated by pairs of stair towers wrapped with glass block and ended in half-cylinders, it offers a welcome formal relief to the flat surfaces of the dormitory slabs. It also serves the practical function of providing a large number of building entrances from an exterior space that can easily be provided with security. As Robert Siegel has explained, "At Columbia now you have enormous buildings with the guards sitting downstairs checking everybody; the kids hate it. So we said: let's secure an outdoor space, and from this space we can have as many entrances as we want."

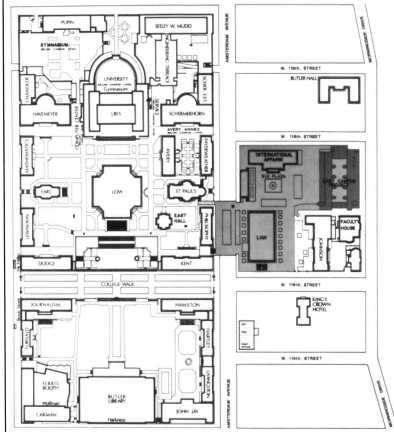

*Right: The new dormitory complex for Columbia solves problems of circulation and unit variety with a straightforward cloister-centered plan and a complex building section. Problems of relating a large, new building mass to smaller neighbors are also addressed. Here the southwest corner of the complex is seen from the bridge to the main campus.*

*Left: Columbia University site plan with the East Campus dormitory shaded at right.*

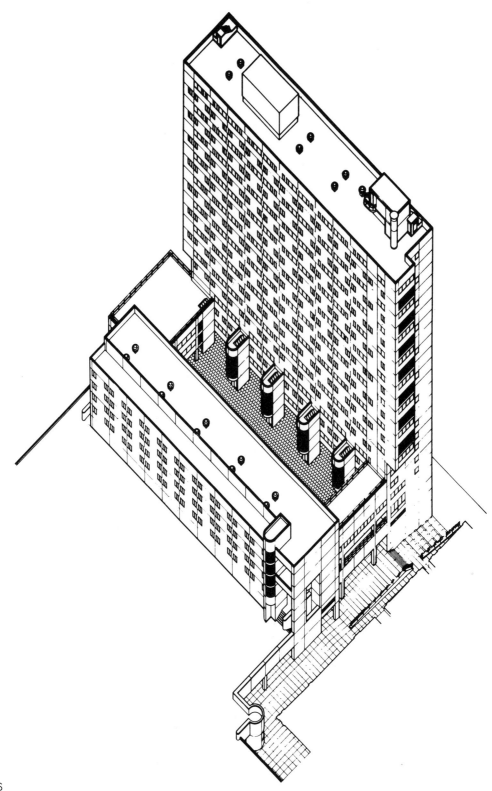

*Left: Axonometric of East Campus dormitory, looking northeast from main campus.*

*Right: Tall slab facing Morningside Park; dark brick of lower floors refers to height of earlier buildings.*

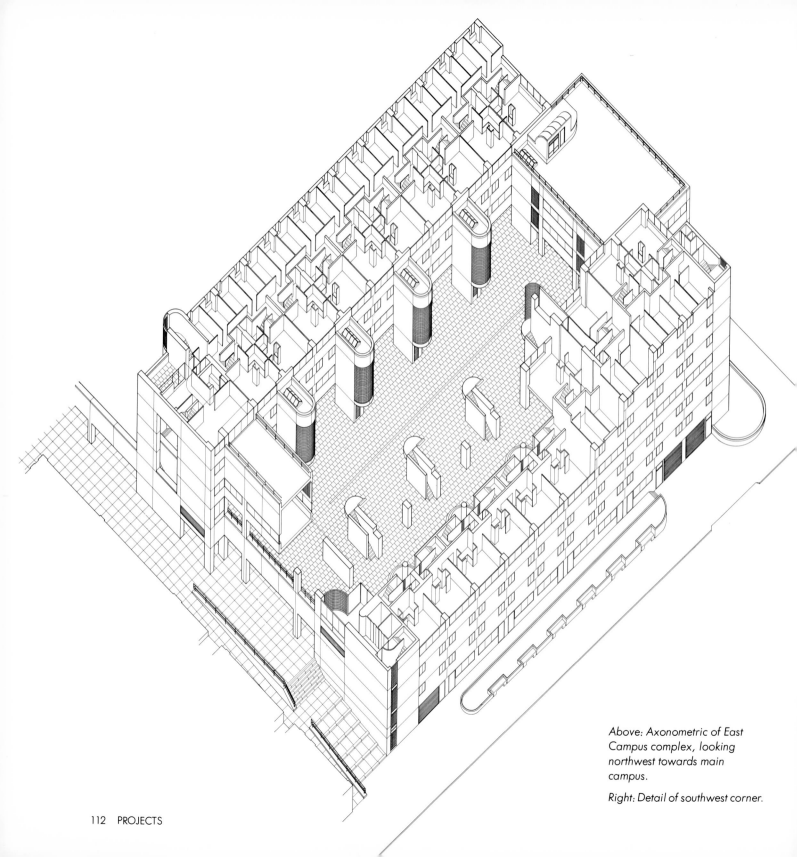

Above: Axonometric of East Campus complex, looking northwest towards main campus.

Right: Detail of southwest corner.

# Long Island House

We close this selection with a Gwathmey Siegel design that is not yet built but that seems likely to be a milestone in the firm's work, not only a summary of many of the experimental efforts of the previous decade, but also a herald of achievement to come.

A large house in eastern Long Island for an anonymous client, it will face south to the Atlantic Ocean across a private expanse of dunes. The approach from the north will be through a wooded site, then along a pond, a tennis court, and a separate structure for servants' quarters. Beyond a motor court, the entrance facade is to have a three-floor-high greenhouse structure as its main feature, but the part of the facade immediately encountered is largely solid, dramatically punctured by a double-height entrance recess. To the east, a stucco wall enclosing a swimming pool area is to be bordered by a long reflecting pool.

For this house Gwathmey Siegel are returning to the natural cedar siding of their earliest houses, but the general palette of materials here is to be richer than ever before: cherry cabinet-work, black granite floors outside and inside, terraces paved with green Vermont slate, and a selection throughout of strong colors coding the exposed greenhouse frame, the pipe rails, the chimney element, and some of the plaster and stucco walls.

But it is the composition of the Long Island house that is most striking, unified on the exterior as few recent works of Gwathmey Siegel have been, but with a highly compartmentalized interior. Although there promise to be long views through and across the house and a fair share of large, interesting, interlocking volumes, it is obvious that the programmatic requirements of the house precluded anything approaching an open plan. Spatial distinctions and provisions for privacy were made in the Cincinnati house by physical separation, but here the elements of the Cincinnati plan have been unified; a number of discrete areas are juxtaposed here, almost like a row of townhouses with party walls.

The resultant effect is composure — not only in the sense of good arrangement, but also in the sense of calm self-possession. Having accommodated complexities and refinements never imagined in the Amagansett houses or the Cogan house, the Long Island house nevertheless returns to the singularity of those early works. It is to be comprehended as one whole object.

What happier ending for a book than this: to predict that this most recent Gwathmey Siegel design will prove to be their strongest, most compelling, most authoritative so far. It makes us eager for the next decade of Gwathmey Siegel architecture.

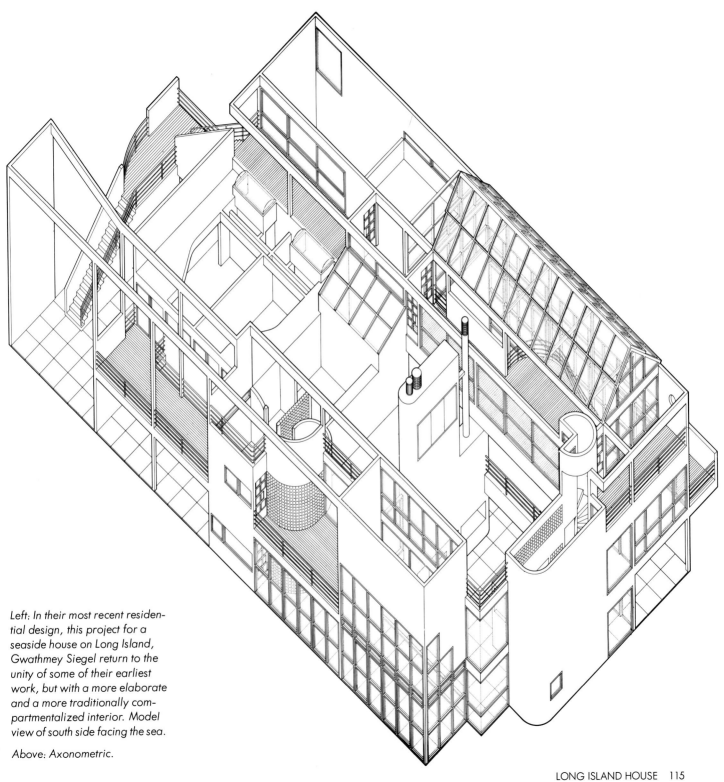

Left: In their most recent residential design, this project for a seaside house on Long Island, Gwathmey Siegel return to the unity of some of their earliest work, but with a more elaborate and a more traditionally compartmentalized interior. Model view of south side facing the sea.

Above: Axonometric.

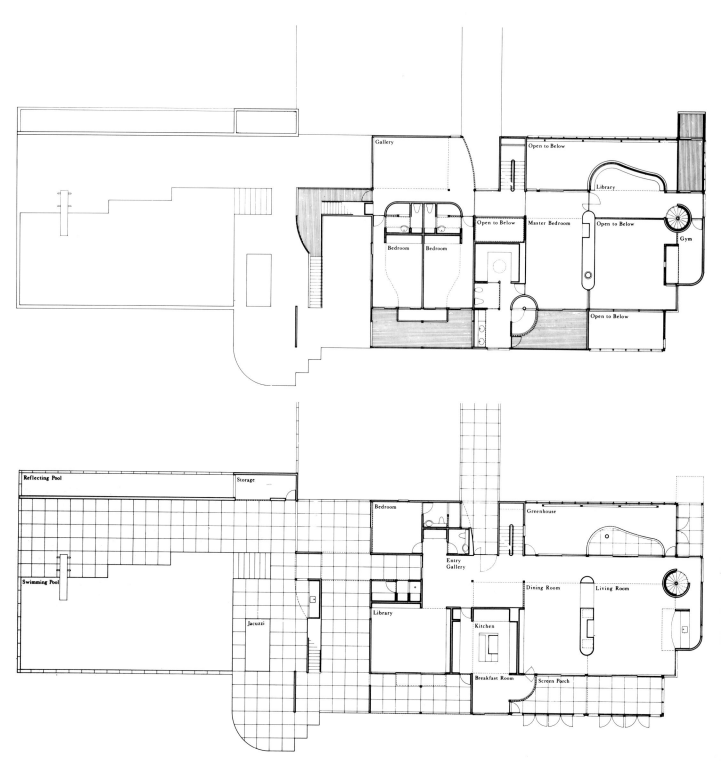

Gallery

Open to Below

Library

Open to Below

Master Bedroom

Open to Below

Gym

Bedroom

Bedroom

Open to Below

Reflecting Pool

Storage

Bedroom

Greenhouse

Swimming Pool

Entry
Gallery

Dining Room

Living Room

Jacuzzi

Library

Kitchen

Breakfast Room

Screen Porch

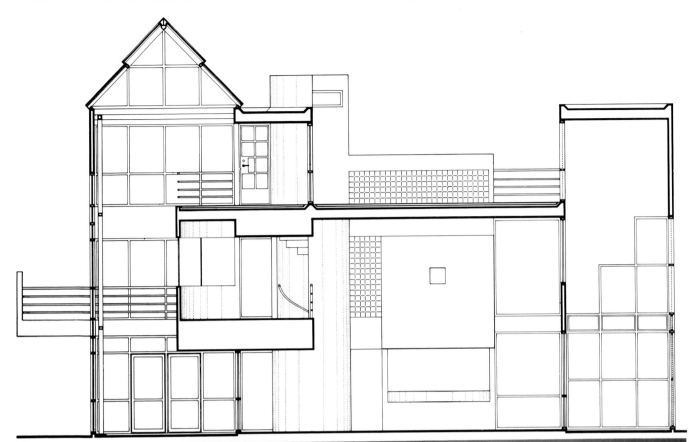

Left: Plans of ground floor (below) and second floor (above) of Long Island house.

Above: Section looking east through greenhouse, living room, and screened porch.

Right: Model of west corner.

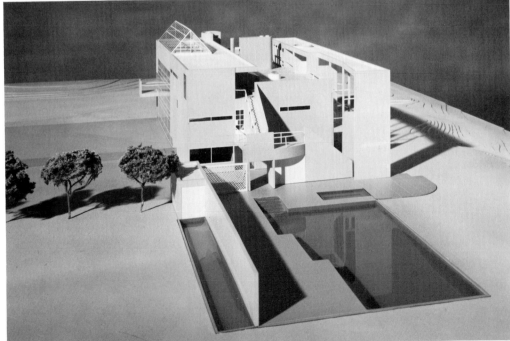

# Chronology

The work of Gwathmey Siegel Architects is listed in the following order for each year: residences, institutions, housing, commercial buildings, interiors. Those works that were designed but unbuilt are indicated with (Project). All dates represent the year of design; completion dates vary from one to five years.

## 1964

Miller Residence*
Fire Island, New York

Neikrug Gallery
New York, New York

## 1965

Gwathmey Residence*
Amagansett, New York

Herlinger Bristol Ltd.
Offices
New York, New York

## 1966

Gwathmey Studio*
Amagansett, New York

Straus Residence*
Purchase, New York

## 1967

Sedacca Residence*
East Hampton, New York

## 1968

Goldberg Residence*
Manchester, Connecticut

Cooper Residence*
Orleans, Massachusetts

## 1969

Bridgehampton Residence I
Bridgehampton, New York

Bridgehampton Residence II
Bridgehampton, New York

Dunaway Apartment
New York, New York

Service Group & Boiler Plant†
State University College
Purchase, New York

New York City Housing Authority
Coney Island Housing
Brooklyn, New York
(Project)

## 1970

Eskilson Residence
Roxbury, Connecticut
(Project)

Tolan Residence
Amagansett, New York

## 1971

Cogan Residence
East Hampton, New York

Elia Bash Residence
Clifton, New Jersey

Breslow Apartment
New York, New York

Dormitory & Dining—
Student Union Facility†
State University College
Purchase, New York

Whig Hall Student Center
Princeton University
Princeton, New Jersey

## 1972

Brooklyn Friends School
Brooklyn, New York

Edgemont School Gymnasium
Scarsdale, New York
(Project)

The Urban Development
Corporation
St. Casimir Housing
Yonkers, New York
(Project)

The Urban Development
Corporation
Low Rise Housing
Lewisboro, New York
(Project)

The Urban Development
Corporation
Low Rise Housing
Sommers, New York
(Project)

Pearl's Restaurant
New York, New York

## 1973

Cohn Residence
Amagansett, New York

Friday Barn
Greenwich, Connecticut

Geffen Residence
Malibu, California
(Project)

Sagner Residence
West Orange, New Jersey
(Project)

Transammonia Corporation
Corporate Offices
New York, New York

Vidal Sassoon Salon
La Costa, California

## 1974

Charof Residence
Montauk, New York

Unger Apartment
New York, New York

Kislevitz Residence
West Hampton, New York

Buettner Residence
Sloatsburg, New York

## 1975

Nassau County Center
for the Arts
Roslyn, New York
(Project)

New York Friends School
Kindergarten
New York, New York

Student Apartment Housing
State University College
Purchase, New York

The Urban Development
Corporation
Whitney Road Housing
Perinton, New York

The Hyatt Corporation
Hotel & Casino
Aruba, Netherlands Antilles
(Project)

The Evans Partnership
Office Building I
Piscataway, New Jersey

Damson Oil Corporation
Office Building
Houston, Texas

The Evans Partnership
Office Building II
Piscataway, New Jersey

Bower & Gardner
Law Offices
New York, New York

Vidal Sassoon
Corporate Offices
Los Angeles, California

U.S. Steakhouse Restaurant
New York, New York

Vidal Sassoon Salon
New York, New York

1976

Fairfax County Department
of Housing
Island Walk Cooperative
Housing
Reston, Virginia

International Energy
Office Building
Houston, Texas

Thomas & Betts Corporation
Laboratory—Office Building
Raritan, New Jersey

Vidal Sassoon Salon
Chicago, Illinois

Vidal Sassoon Salon
Atlanta, Georgia

Blum Hellman Gallery
New York, New York

1977

Swid Apartment
New York, New York

Haupt Residence
Amagansett, New York

Weitz Residence
Quogue, New York

Benenson Residence
Rye, New York

East Campus Housing &
The Heyman Academic Center
Columbia University
New York, New York

The Urban Development
Corporation
Northgate Housing
Roosevelt Island,
New York, New York
(Project)

Northpoint Office Building
Houston, Texas

Amax Petroleum Corporation
Office Building
Houston, Texas

The Evans Partnership
Office Building
Parsippany, New Jersey

Knoll International
Showroom & Office Building
Boston, Massachusetts

Barber Oil Corporation
Corporate Offices
New York, New York

Swirl Incorporated
Showroom & Offices
New York, New York

General Motors Acceptance
Corporation Offices
Brooklyn, New York

Garey Shirtmakers
Incorporated
Showroom & Offices
New York, New York

Posters Originals Limited
Gallery
New York, New York

Shezan Restaurant
New York, New York

Vidal Sassoon Salon
Beverly Hills, California

1978

Geffen Apartment
New York, New York

Crowley Residence
Greenwich, Connecticut

Taft Residence
Cincinnati, Ohio

Westover School
Library & Science Building
Middlebury, Connecticut

Yeshiva University
Belkin Memorial Library
New York, New York

The Columbus Housing Authority
Elderly Housing
Columbus, Indiana

The Columbus Housing Authority
Pence Street Housing
Columbus, Indiana

Colorforms Incorporated
Office & Factory Building
Ramsey, New Jersey

Triangle Pacific Corporation
Corporate Headquarters
Building
Dallas, Texas

A.T.T. Long Lines
Office Building
Parsippany, New Jersey

The Greenwich Savings Bank
New York, New York

General Mills Corporation
Offices
New York, New York

Lincoln Center for the
Performing Arts
Administrative Offices
New York, New York

The Evans Partnership
Corporate Offices
New York, New York

F.D.M. Productions
Offices
New York, New York

The Evans Partnership
Offices
Parsippany, New Jersey

Trammo Petroleum Corporation
Offices
New York, New York

Giorgio Armani
Showroom & Offices
New York, New York

John Weitz Store
Chicago, Illinois

1979

De Menil Residence
Houston, Texas

Hines Residence
Martha's Vineyard, Massachusetts
(Project)

Block Residence
Wilmington, North Carolina
(Project)

De Menil Residence
East Hampton, New York

Viereck Residence
Amagansett, New York

The Evans Partnership
Office Building
Montvale, New Jersey

Ally & Gargano Incorporated
Offices
New York, New York

Morton L. Janklow Associates
Offices
New York, New York

John Weitz Store
New York, New York

1980

Kaufman Residence
Woodbridge, Connecticut

The Greenhill School
Lower School Building
Dallas, Texas
(Project)

The Eastern Long Island
Regional Art Center
Brookhaven, New York
(Project)

The First City Bank
Office Building
Houston, Texas

Bach & Company
Office & Warehouse Building
(Project)

Westbelt Office Building
Houston, Texas
(Project)

The Reliance Group
Corporate Offices
New York, New York

The Fisher Brothers
Corporate Offices
New York, New York

Einstein Moomjy
Showroom
New York, New York

Lincoln Center for the
Performing Arts
Concourse
New York, New York

1981

Donahue Apartment
New York, New York
(Project)

De Menil Residence
New York, New York
(Project)

The Wick Alumni Center
University of Nebraska
Lincoln, Nebraska
(Winner of Competition)

The Westport Public Library
Westport, Connecticut
(Project)

The Evans Partnership
Office Building
Paramus, New Jersey
(Project)

The Evans Partnership
Office Building
Rutherford, New Jersey
(Project)

*By the firm of Gwathmey & Henderson.

†By the firm of Gwathmey, Henderson & Siegel.

## CREDITS

All photographs and drawings courtesy of Gwathmey Siegel Architects.

Otto Baitz: 91— 95, 97, 98 (above), 99— 101
Louis Checkman: 34
David Franzen: 32— 33
Nathaniel Lieberman: 117 (below)
Norman McGrath: 21, 24 (right), 25, 44— 45, 46 (above), 48— 49, 51— 55,
57— 59, 61— 65, 69, 79, 81— 83, 85— 89
Bill Maris: 15, 18— 19, 24 (left), 38— 39, 41— 43, 66, 68
Richard Payne, AIA: 70— 71, 103— 107, 109, 111, 113
Ezra Stoller: 26— 27, 30— 31, 67
Steve Rosenthal: 72, 74— 75, 81